MW01048519

Creatively You

Floral Anti–Stress

Adult Coloring Book

Sue Messruther

Dedication

To my lovely daughter for all of her inspiration,

help and support in the making of this printed garden

Floral Inspirations

This book was designed for those who remember how much fun it was to color in.

The idea for this book came from the lovely people I sometimes sit with who are now in their golden years and many have disabilities, which prevent them from remembering and doing lots of things that they once enjoyed. Watching them color and the enjoyment they felt as they relaxed and focused on their own creations was an amazing experience and gave me the idea that others could enjoy!

How to use this book

This book was designed so you can color on one side only just in case felt tips or whatever you are using bleed through to the other side.

In addition, it is ok if you want to cut your pages out, if you would like to show me your creative colors please take a photo of your work and post it on my Facebook page at https://www.facebook.com/suemessruther.author

How Does Coloring Help to De-Stress?

Do you remember as a child happy you felt when you were coloring in? How many endless hours and how many creations you freely colored in, and then one day you stopped! Well it is time to pick up those crayons and pencils again and de-stress and allow the colors to flow and magically generate a quietness and wellness within you as the colors stimulate your brain but how does this happen?

Glad you asked, when you are coloring in you are using different parts of your brains on one side it is logic and the other is creativity as you focus on your coloring you soon forget whatever is worrying you as you allow your imagination to roam free taking you back to a stress free period of happiness. While you are coloring in you are using your fine motor skills — sounds kind of odd doesn't it but these are what we need to control the pencil /crayon that your using and as you age you lose this skill if you don't continue to practice it.

A weed is only a flower out of place

Because hearts just scroll on

Spreading the love around the garden

Ring a ring a posy

Wall flowers

He loves me he loves me not he loves me!

Fields of flowers

Singing gardens

Wild flowers full of adventure

Copy and compliments

Hidden life beneath the flower beds

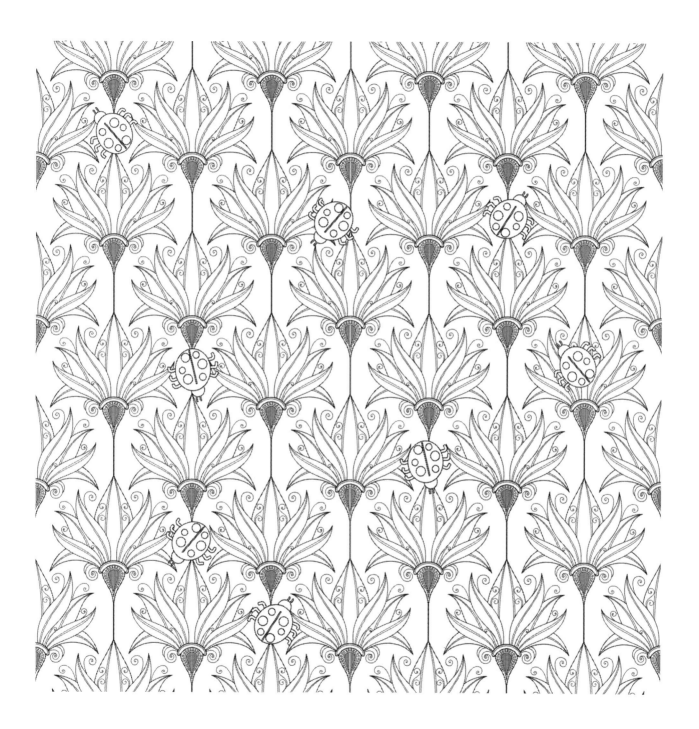

Just for ewe

Perfumed gardens

Tying knots around the flowers

The weave of the garden

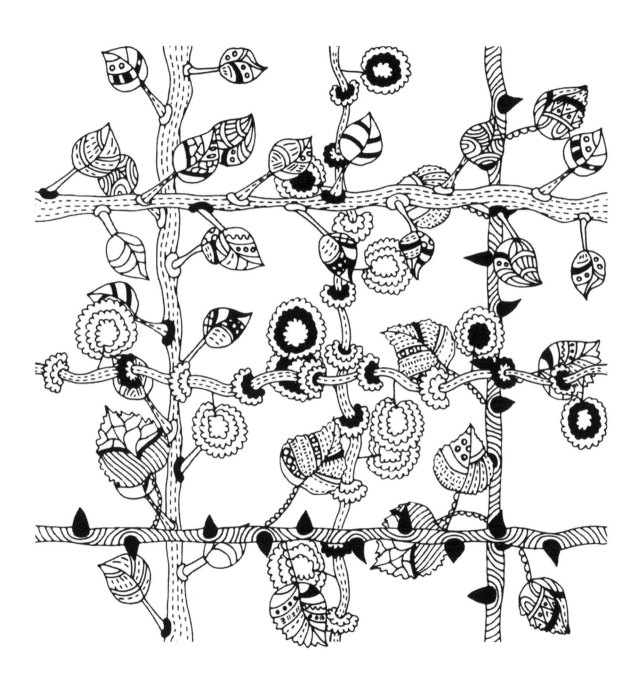

Sun flowers greeting the sky

Doodles of pansies

Dahlias and daisies forever corner

Snails that break your heart

Shady green havens

Living bouquet

Grandma's corner

Bursting seed heads sow next year's glory

Composts so sweet of things that have past

Cacti storing the gardens goodness

Pots of colors glowing in the patio

Blow the little seed heads and make a wish

Tropical beauty a world of its own

Amass with flowers no lawn in sight

About the Author

Born in Adelaide, South Australia, Sue Messruther has written many well-reviewed books, many of them for children. Her bestselling children's volume sets include the *Just For Kids series, Alien Caper Encounters series* and the *Dogs, Cats & All Other Animals.*

Messruther's stand-alone titles are *Santa's Christmas: The Year the Sleigh Broke Down, Christmas Home Made Cookie Gifts,* and *30 Best Breads From Around the World.*

Messruther has also contributed writings to the books *Thorns to be Thankful For* and *Skill Share* both of which became best sellers in the first week of publication.

A new children's series, **Play Time Books**, is forthcoming from the author, of which *Come Find Me Under The Sea* will be its first title followed by *Back In Time With Dinosaurs* and then *It's A Dog's Life.* Titles after this are yet to be determined!

Messruther has lived in Cairns, Queensland Australia and now currently resides in Scarborough, North Yorkshire, England, with her family and Oscar, an Old English Sheep puppy of gigantic proportions, (Digby is a constant thought and fear, and will Oscar grow that big!).

Other Titles

Just For Kids Series

Vol 1: Kids in the kitchen who are having fun creating

Vol 2: Kids in the kitchen who are creatively baking

Vol 3: Kids in the kitchen cooking up a storm

Dogs, Cats & All Other Animals

If Puppies Could Talk

If kittens could talk........ What would they say?

If Rabbits Could Talk

Stand Alone Books

Santa's Christmas - The year Santa's sleigh broke down

Alien Capers Encounters Series

Book 1: Sock Seekers

Book 2: Underwear, Underpants

Book 3: Vanishing Walking Shoes

Book 4: Out of World Hat Parade

Coming Soon

Play Time Books

Come Find Me Under The Sea

Back In Time With Dinosaurs

It's A Dog's Life

Printed in Great Britain
by Amazon